47 Incantatory Essays

Poems by Stefene Russell

Kansas City   Spartan Press   Missouri

Spartan Press
Kansas City, Missouri
spartanpresskc.com

Copyright (c) Stefene Russell, 2018
First Edition 1 3 5 7 9 10 8 6 4 2
ISBN: 978-1-946642-95-0
LCCN: 2018914990

Design, edits and layout: Jason Ryberg
Cover image: Philip P. Betts
Author photo: Kevin A. Roberts
All rights reserved. No part of this publication may be reproduced or transmitted in any form or by any means, electronic or mechanical, including photocopying, recording or by info retrieval system, without prior written permission from the author.

Spartan Press would like to thank Prospero's Books, The Fellowship of N-finite Jest, The Prospero Institute of Disquieted P/o/e/t/i/c/s, Will Leathem, Tom Wayne, Jeanette Powers, j. d. tulloch, Jon Bidwell, Jason Preu, Mark McClane, Tony Hayden and the whole Osage Arts Community.

Poem No. 10 and Poem No. 47 appeared in the winter 2019 edition of *Otis Nebula* (otisnebula.com).

Title page image courtesy of the Metropolitan Museum of Art, via a Creative Commons Zero (CCO) license. Allen & Ginter Cigarette card, 1887, The Jefferson R. Burdick Collection, Gift of Jefferson R. Burdick (Accession Number 63.350.201.6.24).

Resemblances to persons living or dead may not be purely coincidental; "I" poems are not autobiographical, but come from the mythic/connective unconscious "I" (and/or the Historical Newspapers Database). Also, some of this research and material originally appeared in a different format in history columns for *St. Louis Magazine*.

CONTENTS

He took trains back when the station was busy / 1
There was a bad dip in the alley in back of school / 2
Your mother's mother / 4
Your mother's mother or your father's mother / 6
Your cousin found the photo album in your
    aunt's garage / 8
Your very old neighbor, in his mustard-colored
    Van Heusen shirt / 10
Your great-uncle and your great-aunt lived out
    in the country / 12
Dads and lawns and lawns and dads / 14
Do you remember V-8 engines? / 16
What the grass says in Kaskaskia is not what the grass
    says in Cascade / 18
There went the doorbell / 20
Your grandparents always went to that fancy
    supper club / 21
Everyone wanted to be in those little clubs
    when Jeanne Trevor sang / 22
Your weird cousin / 24
The motorcycle clubs passed it on their way
    to Shady Jack's bar / 26
It opened a few days before Christmas 1875 / 28
Hyde Park Beer is the beer of your fathers / 30
You think Granite City is named after the rock / 31
It's a sepia photograph of your relatives, dancing / 32
On New Year's Day, a day I spent stuffing straw
    into a Styrofoam cooler / 34
Blessed are the pie-bakers of Chicago / 36
Ages ago, during a winter back when it snowed / 37
The fifth of July is a holiday but no one will admit it / 38
Greyhound's Streamline Moderne buses weren't
    any faster / 40

In the morning, they resurfaced the rink / 41
They call it fanning / 42
Fabric stores / 44
Barn swallows don't need barns / 46
Ice sings when it melts and freezes and shifts / 47
Back in the day, it was easy for the son of a Prussian
    shepherd to make it big in the drug business / 48
Walt Whitman wrote poems about bridges, trains,
    and telegraph lines / 50
Madam Z., Mr. Z's wife, read cards and palms
    at the Egyptian Tea Room / 52
An old-timey livery stable seems so wholesome / 54
A long time ago, Famous-Barr kept artists
    on its payroll / 56
Back then the sky turned a different color / 58
All that blue pouring from the windows / 59
The International Ladies' Garment Workers' Union
    threw a Christmas party for their kids / 61
When your grandmother visited from California / 62
If the '70s had never happened / 64
Pull out the wedding album / 66
This is the year sugar rationing ended / 68
A long time ago every big city had another little city
    within it / 70
Black and green clouds rolled into the city, punctuated
    by scratches of lightning / 72
Lambs arriving at the East St. Louis stockyards / 73
This is a picture of my neighbor's father / 74
If it had retained its original name, no one would play
    trombone in high school / 75
There's a tiny star splinter stuck in Jennifer's eye / 76

*O words are poor receipts for what time
hath stole away.*

—John Clare, *Poems Chiefly From Manuscript*

1.

He took trains back when the station was busy, when one man's job was scraping gum off the floor. He took trains in a station packed with salesmen saying goodbye as wives cried and waved goodbye with air kisses or chiffon hankies. He took buses, a symphony called *Venery* playing on the P.A., over and over. He took trains from Illinois to California and back again. He took trains, making excuses and never saying goodbye. He leaned his head on a window, slept with his hat on, counted cows in Iowa. He ate no food, drank only coffee. He sat in the dining car, watching Amish farmers play cards. He took trains to find places with neon signs, places with names like The It Club. He took trains to dizzy himself with drinks and floorshows, to see ladies in red dresses and ridiculous glittering shoes. He took trains and lit ladies' cigarettes with a silver-tipped match from a book whose cover bore a photo of the bar he now stood in. He took trains to escape a life of safety matches with their red brick tips and a future stacking bricks. He waited for a train at midnight, cigarettes in one pocket and cigarettes in the other. He waited for the train in an empty station, no company but the ghosts of Harvey girls, blowing through arched hallways, blowing over benches, clutching at their glowing toothaches and headaches, with ghost bows in their ghost hair. He had nothing to say to them and nothing better to do but stare and think and think and stare until the train pulled in.

2.

There was a bad dip in the alley in back of school and it
filled with water and the water froze. All the boys in the
neighborhood went down there and pretended to skate,
skating in their shoes, imagining blades on the bottom
of their feet. The fake skate rink was a short walk from
Mr. G.'s bar. He really had a history back home, wherever
it was he came from, and his bar wasn't really a bar.
The neighborhood gossip found the body of a murder-
trial witness, wrapped rope and blankets, dumped in an
ash pit near Biddle Market. Biddle Market where Mamie
Green worked, Mamie who dated a guy who was 30,
Mamie who worked at a fruit stall. Mamie who came to
work one morning and drank a bottle of Paris Green.
Mamie who lived near the Two Annies, Howard and Hanes.
The Annies of Cass Avenue. Homeless Annies because the
city came and tore down their building. Annies who yelled
when anyone said they should go to the poorhouse. Annies
who built a hut out of tin and burlap and pallets with
a gunnysack flag flying on the roof. Annies who cooked
dandelions and vegetables thrown out at Biddle Market.
Annies at leisure in a neighborhood full of anarchists,
brickbats, mule wranglers, burlap-bag menders, professional
rat-catchers. Home to Spider Meyers, King of the Daggers.
Home to Stolle Hall, where Frankie shot Johnnie.
A place where gray horses turned green on St. Patrick's Day.
A place of storefront synagogues and apartment bakeries.
Home to bon-bon dippers and coffin-tassel twisters.
Home to Oscar Berger, champion goose-driver. Home to
Oscar Berger who spread pitch and sand in his yard and
marched the geese through to *put a sole on their foot.*

Oscar who led geese through downtown to market at 4 a.m. with an eerie whistle he learned during his youth in the countryside. A place that's a magnet for sanitary inspectors. Inspectors who told the newspaper we were the plague spot of America. Plague inspectors who told the paper our houses were too dark, too narrow, too full of people. Inspector chased by an old housewife with a knife. Inspector bringing cop friends. Inspector taking to jail the lovely Mr. Z., who everyone knew, who sang as he stirred his barrel of what he called *California wine.* Mr. Z, stirring and stirring with his wine-stained broom handle. Mr. Z signing sad songs into his California wine. Mr. Z, who never set foot in California. Mr. Z who corked up his songs with his wine in old vinegar bottles, left on our doorsteps at Christmas, gone by Epiphany.

3.
Your mother's mother, or your mother's mother's mother. Bettys and Joys and Junes and Bevs. Shampoo sets and slip-covered microscopes. They called them probies. Probationary nursing students. They studied biology for five months, then social science, then anatomy. They labeled the organs of a rubber Adonis without arms or legs. A dreamboat guy who was just a torso, whose organs were out there for everyone to see. A handsome gent who, were he animate, would shriek over his lack of clothes, skin, eyelids. A flayed Adonis shouting, hey, you can see my liver! Hey, don't look at my gallbladder like that! The probies took out all his organs and put them back again, probies in jade green dresses with button-on aprons and bibs and a little half-moon hat. Before Vatican II, before Albion Fairs and Woodstock and back to the land, when you had to study Latin in high school even if you weren't Catholic, a nurse's uniform was a shrunken nun's habit. Before Florence Nightingale invented nursing school, it was all up to the nuns. Nuns washing plague bodies and nuns carrying bodies pocked with sores, piggybacking the dead to hallowed ground. When you shucked the jade green smock you graduated to all-white, dearest bride of the sick ward. Every night you came home, drew a little bleach bath in the sink for your uniform and stockings. You polished your white oxfords with Sani-White. You double-checked your jar full of bobby pins to make sure you could anchor your white cap to your curls. Maybe it's all David Bowie's fault. Those zip-up smocks

that came into fashion after that, made for either a he or
she. Then everyone, everyone in the same scrubs, blue or
jade. Some scientist somewhere studied why little
children are terrified of people dressed all in white.
Go tell that to your mother's mother, who used to be a
nurse. Go tell that to David Bowie. Go tell that to Jesus.

4.

Your mother's mother or your father's mother or your mother's father will tell you, when they bought clothes, it wasn't like now. You didn't put your new socks and your new shirt in the same cart with the washing detergent and a vanilla candle and tin of protein powder and a pair of shoes and jumper cables and soda and vodka and bananas and kombucha and a paperweight and beef jerky and a lamp and a bag of dog food and hey! Cute Socks, run through with sparkle thread. Buying clothes, it was practically a public holiday, they say. Back then it was. You got on a bus with your mother. You went to a department store in late August, when you could still feel rivulets of sweat running down your back in the heat. You looked at tartan skirts or wool trousers, clothes you'd rather die than wear right then. Everything was wrapped in tissue paper, boxed, tucked away on a high shelf till the first day of school. Those boxes signaled the need to start coping with the fact that summer was over. But it also charged up those new outfits with a kind of specialness. Boyd's, Woolworth's, and Famous-Barr, every year they had a parade downtown and you saw the clothes you couldn't buy yet. And in the newspapers and in your mailbox, you saw clothes you couldn't buy yet. So when you wore them, it felt like they came out of a dream. Maybe they did. Maybe you did have a dream about those clothes. That pair of shoes, that dress, that shirt, all charged up like they fell out of a cloud. It was a power, that first day of school. You got to say, this is who I am now. Last year you took me for a loser. I am entering the building on the first day of class wearing *yellow.* Wearing *purple.* Wearing gold shoes. All bets are off, you sorry so-and-sos!

5.

Your cousin found the photo album in your aunt's garage. In it there's a photograph of a bad dream. A postcard. A picture of a room full of pipes. A room full of holes. A room full of places to fall into. A picture of the brickworks, the clay pits in North St. Louis, where they made bricks and terra cotta sewer pipes. They put the pipes underground but the pipes used to *be* the ground. Red Missouri clay, *terra cocta,* cooked earth. The immigrants knew it was an ancestor material, forever and ever used for roof tiles and cooking pots and Venuses of Willendorf. In 1910, North City was all open clay pits and brickyards and terra-cotta works. The kilns they used were round, like a gnome's hut. They built it from the same bricks it cooked to hardness, its furnace fed with coal mined not far from the clay beds. There were shelves inside, and if you opened the door it looked like a weird little library stocked with petrified books. The holes in North City grew deeper as guys dug and pickaxed veins of clay and mined coal and carted wheelbarrows of fired or unfired bricks in and out of sweltering kilns. St. Louis got taller as architects married steel frames with bricks, and the terra-cotta ornaments grew fancier, with Celtic knots and basket weaves and interlocking vegetal patterns. And then here came Le Corbusier with his white buildings that were really machines. St. Louis, with your French roots, you fell for it. You felled the old buildings. Traded them for white boxes in the International Style. Traded them for cheap boxes in the American style. White boxes and gray boxes and brown boxes. *Look at this terrible place,* the people said, *it's literally built out of dirt.* And the children of the children of the children now make a sport out of longing for everything long-gone, weeping over fire maps that say used to be a clay mine, the Arrow No. 1 mine and the Gittens Mine and the Coffin Mine, marked out in clean, scored lines, painted canary yellow and bismuth pink.

6.

Your very old neighbor, in his mustard-colored Van Heusen shirt, plaid polyester pants, and horn-rimmed glasses, stood in the alley, burning leaves in a metal garbage can. The world smelled like smoke and dead leaves and meatloaf and the static leaping off of wool blankets. Your grandmother sent a Halloween card from California, a Halloween cat with a giant head, eyes and teeth traced with glow-in-the-dark ink, fine silver glitter instead of fur. Somehow it all left you feeling like something big was about to happen, bigger than Halloween, or your mother sitting at a sewing machine, piecing together a Butterick pioneer costume. Bigger than walking around with a pillowcase and asking for candy, walking with your sisters through neighborhoods you knew and ones you didn't know, turning back at midnight because you had reached a clutch of university apartments, where the college kids were at parties and didn't have candy anyway. Some people had parents who stayed home and watched *The Tonight Show* with a candy bowl filled with old people candy, Mallo Bars or Mary Janes. Some kids' parents wore costumes provisioned from old drapes or sailor hats from Disneyland and pulled out of the driveway in a station wagon to go drink, leaving the kids with TV dinners and a babysitter. Some kids went out alone, in store-bought costumes: plastic smocks, always something on TV or in the movies, like Wonder Woman, or an X-wing pilot. The rigid masks had a breathing hole at the mouth, which invited you to stick your tongue through, though you knew you'd taste blood. You believed fairy tales like Snow

White must be kind of true because the adults said you can't have the apples, they have razors in them, or drugs. You knew it wasn't safe to care too much, but you didn't know why. It felt like something very scary had happened to the whole world recently, but no one wanted to talk about it. And hanging in the air like your neighbor's musty leaf smoke, a feeling of unease, uncanny as that radium-green moon pooling light over a sparkling cat, its eyes and teeth glowing in the dark.

7.

Your great-uncle and your great-aunt lived out in the country and their house had a weird smell. It couldn't have been the smell of liver spots but that's what you thought of when you smelled it, their shaky spotty hands. There were no family photos hanging on the walls at all, just things your great-aunt cross-stitched, embroideries of flowers and alphabets and animals. Your great-uncle had a magnifying glass on a metal band he would strap to his bald head when he looked at his stamps. He stored them in see-through envelopes in ammo boxes in his study, where he never opened the drapes. I said, why don't you put them in an album. They're an investment, he said. The glue on the back was shiny and looked pale pink. I always wanted so bad to lick them and put them on something. I couldn't figure out how people had resisted licking and sticking them, even if just for a letter. He had a special box with special stamps in it, he said you couldn't send letters with these ones. He said they were Helmar stamps, and I said, who is Helmar. He said Helmar was not a person. Helmar was a type of cigarette, made a very long time ago, when a pack of smokes only cost 10 cents. But it wasn't a pack of smokes, they came in cardboard clamshell, folded under gold paper. Under the paper you found a glassine envelope that said *Smoke HELMAR cigarettes/and carry your/ POSTAGE STAMPS/in this envelope./THEY WILL NOT STICK.* That wasn't true, he said, they did stick. The envelope had cancelled stamps from all over the world and also Helmar stamps. They were just fake stamps with famous people on them, like baseball players. When I was in high school I made the mistake of licking and sticking one, a rare one, and I can't find it now. It was a Frank "Home Run" Baker. But I have almost all the ball players, Red Doonin, Lefty Leifield, Hooks Witse. Joe Lake, who pitched for the Browns. Steve Evans, I don't know why they called him Steve, his name was Louis. Left-handed, pitched for the Cards, ended his career with the Terrapins in Baltimore. They had ones with actresses on them, too, he said, people no one remembers now. I never did much go in much for the movie stars, he said.

8.

Dads and lawns and lawns and dads. America, you think about those two things all the time, at least you say you do. Throw some cans of beer in there for flourish. Cutting grass is a warrior sport that evolved from a landed gentry sport. Cutting grass fast came from a daydream. The guy who invented lawnmowers wasn't thinking about lawns. He was looking at velvet. His name was Edward; he lived in England. He was, for some reason, standing in a textile mill, watching a machine shave the fuzz off fabric. It made him think about grass. In 1827, the year that Edward stood inside a textile mill watching a machine shave the fuzz off fabric, the only way to cut grass was to whistle your servants over and put scythes in their hands and point at the grass. Now the scythes were hung on pegs in the barn and left there forevermore. The Coldwell Lawn Mower, with its excellent network of flywheels, water chambers, and greasy chains, could blow through an acre of grass in an hour. Armies of servants rolled clumsy proto-push mowers *across the vegetable surfaces of lawns, grass-plats, and pleasure grounds.* Americans decided they wanted vegetable surfaces for their pleasure grounds, too. They plowed the prairie under for fescue, unrolling sod for tennis courts and football fields, all the while talking about how grass grew great in America even though it hardly grew at all. They didn't care that it would be all about blades and poison. They didn't care that it would be a war. There's an encyclopedia that documents all the world's secrets. Look up "C.W." That stands for *chemical warfare.* That entry cites a place where you can go online to watch a video. It has animated charts and graphs. You watch a dot go *blip blip blip* back and forth, a pixelated metal canister thrown across no man's land, leaking Agent Orange, 2,4-D and DDT. A little silver bomb spitting broken lines that talks about wars and lawns, and lawns and wars, and dads and lawns, and wars and dads.

9.

Do you remember V-8 engines? Uniforms without sleeve patches? Six-shot .38s, mutton-chop sideburns, polyester pants with white piping? Those were the questions put to the readers of *Gendarme,* the St. Louis Police Officers' Association newsletter. *If you answered yes*, it said, *you know Grand Fuzz*. In the early 1970s, three St. Louis City cops, including William "Wild Bill" Vicente, a monster on the Hammond B-3, started a cop band. Fans of Grand Funk Railroad, as you can see. The members stated their genre as "Footstompin' Music" a la *E Pluribus Funk.* They wanted to play in high schools, to get all those long-haired kids to see them as guys, not pigs. Or at least cool pigs. They rehearsed in lead singer Barry Lalumandier's basement. Sporadically, though; they all worked different shifts. Grand Fuzz got its first big break with a gig at the Police Athletic League picnic at the Pipefitters complex on Larimore Road in July 1974. The cliché is don't quit your day job. These cops quit their day jobs. Grand Fuzz didn't patrol anymore. Grand Fuzz headlined the VP Fair. Grand Fuzz got screamed at by girls. Grand Fuzz couldn't pump their own gas without some S.O.B. bugging them for autographs. Grand Fuzz got bags and bags of fan mail. Record companies came calling. And then, it was 1983. Grand Funk Railroad broke up. Teenage girls didn't scream at Grand Fuzz's oldest member, flugelhorn player Elmer Daughtery, who'd just turned 40. Teenage girls wore jelly shoes and rode pink and green scooters and dyed their hair green and pink and screamed at guys who didn't look like guys. No one wanted to hear a

wah-wah pedal anymore. Give us drum machines
and strobe lights and hairspray, they said. Because here
comes the apocalypse, they said. No one's graduating
from high school because here comes the bomb, they
said. No cop will play the last song I hear on earth, they
said. I refuse to go out to the sound of stomping feet.
Give me tangerines soaked in Everclear and cigarettes
and Diamond Dogs and Charlotte Sometimes, they said.

10.
What the grass says in Kaskaskia is not what the grass says in Cascade; what it says in Sugar City is not what it says in Magic City. And what it says in Dog Walk is not what it says in Possum Trot. You think there's no grass in the desert but the grass tells me otherwise. It grows timidly near the edge of burrows, a mumbling gray grass browsed by creatures. Acres of it shimmer behind chain link fences, near faux stucco houses. Grass struck dumb most days. Sober grass that knows its place. Shorn very short. Lovely, we say. The eye doesn't mind but some ancient organ in the soul objects. Even in those who stride across wearing spikes, nine iron in hand. Subdued grass, not tamed grass. Beneath the lawn is lawlessness. The grass on my block is joint-grass, Bermuda grass, crabgrass, clover, chicory, plantain, ragweed, chickweed. Cut ragged. A faux lawn. Once when the city came to mow a man on the crew said look at these grasses, talking trash because they are trash. The trees they grow beneath are trash. But that tree is called a tree of heaven, I said, and it talks like it knows the place. In China, they use it to cure sadness. In China, the mimosa's perfume cures melancholy, and its silvery bark cures melancholy. In America, the pink flowers are trash and the silver bark is trash and messages go uncoded. Wild grass is catching. Wild grass converses with the world like wild yeasts and viruses do, like very little girls do. It colonizes the side of the highway, even in fancy places. Johnsongrass with its musty tassels and the light blue of chicory and yellow polka dots of celandine. Even zoysia has its limits.

In fall, it says: I do not want to. I click my chlorophyll off. Don't feel like it. I slumber. It's cold. Here I go. And I go yellow, yellow, yellow. Not till March do I wake. Or April. Maybe.

11.

There went the doorbell, and the doorbell, and the doorbell: Annie Oakley, Pallas Athena, Gandalf. A man in a powder blue tux, all frills. A couple in sateen druid's robes, papier-mâché eyeballs for heads. The worst question of the night: *what are you supposed to be?* In the dining room, a long table, punchbowls, a bar, some punch drunks. *I'll have a Bee Stinger, a Trick Knee, a Double Rainbow.* A man wearing a tiny roof for a hat. A gold-lamé giraffe. A woman in a rain barrel dancing with a man wearing nothing but a nightshirt. But mostly plain old cavemen, devils, cowboys, clowns, ballerinas, witches, hobos. The last boozy holdouts, stumbling to taxis at 3 a.m. The moon flashing in and out of a bank of fast-moving clouds, the cold acrid air heavy with smoke. Taxis driving past the levee, past the flicker of campfires on the river, blue speckled kettles sputtering over open fires, boiling water for imaginary tea or tea made with stones and weeds. Taxi driving past a crumpled figure on a sidewalk grate, coat fanned out to catch the warmth in the cloud of steam. A drunk man exits a taxi. A drunk man stands in his small kitchen in his small apartment, eating stale bread spread with cold butter just out of the fridge, drinking water right out of the faucet. Drunk man watching his own reflection in the window at 4 a.m., superimposed over the backyard and the widow across the alley in her robe, putting out her trash. Drunk man looking at his reflection in a window: an adult in greasepaint and a funny hat. Drunk man stops chewing to ask himself: *hey, what are you supposed to be?*

12.

Your grandparents always went to that fancy supper club, the place where they kicked you out for not wearing a jacket or a dress, a place where the walls were covered with shiny fabric. A place where they turned the lights very low and put the wine in a wicker sleeve and brought out the meat on a slab of wood. You pointed and hoped for the best, because you didn't know how much you'd just spent. When things went south in the neighborhood, when the discothèques and go-go bars opened, the guys still wore jackets but with skinny ties and slicked-back hair. At the Gilded Cage the women danced in actual cages, not gilded but spray-painted gold, wore sequin bikinis and corsages made out of fur pom-poms dyed to match the color of the sequins. All the young guys still slicked their hair back, but they were letting it grow, hanging greasy behind their ears. The older guys at the bar, they frowned. The in-between guys who fought in Korea. Maybe a newspaper man, or, worse, insurance or real estate, drinking scotch and smoking colored Nat Sherman cigarettes that came in a cardboard clamshell with gold foil paper. When you lifted the foil it was like a peacock made out of cigarettes. The guy who shouldn't drink that much who just kept drinking. He drank and squinted and listened to Farrell's Top 10 parade, the corny strains of "Wooly Bully" mingling with the unbridled hedonism of the Rolling Stones, Bob Dylan's surly poetics and Jackie DeShannon, who told us all the world needed was love.

13.
Everyone wanted to be in those little clubs when Jeanne Trevor sang. She was in the newspaper. The Sunday magazine photographer followed her for days. He photographed her sitting with Peanuts Whalum at a café table outside Karl's Two Cents Plain. He photographed her by the Old Cathedral, with the Arch half-finished in the background. She raised her arms up to fill the shape where the Arch would be. She posed in the doorway of the Opera House Store, with its old-fashioned rosette carpet and hanging Tiffany lamps. She browsed through antique bottles and gazed into a half-lit case decorated with honeycomb tissue-paper globes and fan bursts. She tried on costume jewelry and laughed, wearing oversized, theatrical hats. She hammed it up with a marabou purse as big as a suitcase. The Opera House Store is gone. Even that kind of store is gone, as the rotary phones and old matchbooks go up on eBay, and our every task and impulse finds a way to turn into pixels. There was also a jazz club called the Opera House, but Jeanne sang at Crystal Palace and the Blackhorse Tavern. That bar had a British theme, with a shield and swords hung on the wall, its twilit bar area illuminated with the softly glowing panels of the jukebox and the cigarette machine. She sang with a voice that could take on a diamond shimmer like Ella's, or go deep and wine-colored like Billie's. You could see in the photos her natural disposition is sunny, but when she sings, she sings the whole world, happy and sad: road trips and

fireworks, love letters and lovers' spats, and the feeling of watching dogwood petals helicoptering into the rain gutter, turning from pink to gray, leaving your chest tight with that wistful feeling of watching another spring pass.

14.
Your weird cousin, your bad cousin, your cousin with the shaggy hair who wore an army coat that always smelled like basement dirt, he liked to walk to Katz Drugstore every day. Or to be more specific, he loved beer.
He walked to the Katz on South Grand, the one with the giant neon cat sign on the roof, neon cat with neon whiskers and neon bow tie. It was the same smiling cat you saw on Katz beer cans. They kept some in the freezer and some on the counter. It was 10 cents less for warm beer. Your bad cousin bought the warm beer and drank it on the way home. He flattened the cans, dug up the dirt floor in your uncle's basement, hid them in the hole.
The smiling cat's face was on everything: flashbulbs, jumbo salted peanuts, coffee, powdered sulfur. Katz sold spider monkeys and baby alligators, and bins of 45s, and film-developing kits, and bridge lamps, and *Toujours Moi* perfume and Van Ess hair tonic. Some Katzes had shoe-repair shops. Some of them had photo booths. Some of them had pinball machines and a soda fountain that sold lime ices to go. Katz sold creepy old patent medicines, the ones your farmer grandpa bought: Wampole's Preparation, Paregoric. When you called in your prescription you could tell the pharmacist what flavor to make the cough syrup. Everyone in America loved Katz for its muchness. Because that's so American. Smiling cat beer, everflowing. Pyramids of tobacco tins, rows of lipsticks and celluloid dolls, sleds, soap flakes, tooth powders, roach bait, sleazy magazines, candy bars, mustard plasters. Elvis' first gig was in a Katz parking lot

in Memphis. The everything store. It merged and merged again. Now it's CVS. Your weird cousin is fat now, with a pocket full of sobriety tokens. You can't buy lime ices or baby alligators at CVS but the drugstore's still there. You've never been to Graceland. You never drank warm cat beer. You miss the smiling cat. You miss blackberry-flavored cough syrup. Life is cheap, and it just gets cheaper.

15.
The motorcycle clubs passed it on their way to Shady Jack's bar. If anyone noticed it, it would've been the bikers. A boulder on a plinth. A plinth of chunky rocks assembled (maybe?) by drunken river roustabouts. On the boulder, four screw holes and a big bleached square where the plaque had been. Who knew what it was? Not the bikers. Only the jerk that stole the plaque if he even bothered to look at it on the way to the scrapyard. The other people driving down North Broadway—factory workers heading to Chili Mac's, cheap landscapers buying cheap trees at the wholesale nursery, daytime drunks headed to the East Coast Lounge, singers and true believers headed to the Gospel Choral Union Hall—never noticed it at all. Even though was a big rock on a plinth on a triangle of grass in the middle of North Broadway. Then the state built a new bridge over the Mississippi. They moved the rock on top of a sleek new concrete plinth. They put a plaque on it. The plaque explained this boulder had been placed on North Broadway to commemorate *la grange de terre*, the earth barn, Big Mound. The ghosts down there will tell you, even if the bikers won't, the rock was in the wrong place. That triangle of grass marked the place where the old French Market stood, not the Big Mound. They can't put a rock where Big Mound was; the bridge runs over it. A long time ago Big Mound got picked and shoveled to death, just to use as paving dirt for the railroads. When the French got here, there were 40 burial mounds in St. Louis. Big Mound was so true to its name you could see it on a boat from the

river. That's why they called it the barn of earth. Before leveling it, a cypress-wood coffin worked its way out of the soil. It held a man wrapped in a European blanket, plus some rusty steel bracelets with characters too corroded to read, and a queue of human hair, *about a foot long and plaited, and besmeared with vermilion paint.* An old man called the *Daily Missouri Republican* to report it was *one of the Osagus who'd died of small-pox,* interred there with four other men at the tribe's request. The reporters acknowledged it was a burial site and yet still ran a letter from a professor at the St. Louis Academy of Science who said it was OK to use as fill dirt because it wasn't actually a burial mound. He said Big Mound was just a bunch of silt that built up from the river. Silt that somehow, 25 feet down, held a cache of conch shells, beads, and a skeleton with a skull resting on copper plates *about the thickness of a tablespoon* and bearing a face with a long nose that more *nearly resembles the beak of a bird than the proboscis of a man or animal.* The state sent archaeologists to dig before the new bridge went up. One day they unearthed a clay goddess, squash blossoms in her hair, her hoe sprouting leaves and turning into a serpent. The ground where they found her is paved now. It's paved and there's a gas station there now. A gas station for all the cars driving back and forth over the bridge, whose feet sit right where Big Mound used to be.

16.

It opened a few days before Christmas 1875, at Third and Pine streets. Every hinge and doorknob was brass. It had winding walnut staircases, white marble fountains, a hand-carved walnut rostrum. The vaulted ceiling was covered in flower medallions and murals of figures in cloudscapes, reclining ladies and men on horseback, bearing flags. A huge chalkboard ran down the length of one wall, where clerks wrote, erased, and rewrote prices for corn, bran, soybeans, hogs, and wheat. Buyers inspected grain at marble-topped tables, samples poured into metal bowls, and they'd sniff, squint at, or test kernels between their teeth. Grain flowed into bowls, and money and power flowed in and out of the big rooms. The Veiled Prophet Ball happened there. So did the 1876 Democratic National Convention. In 1901, 500 mayors from all over the world came here for "Centennial Week," to watch the traders on the floor. The rostrum was decorated with *sheaves of corn, wheat, oats, and barley, and at each corner was a pyramid of golden pumpkins… and most wonderful of all, the leader of the band, which played in front of the rostrum, stood on a giant pumpkin.* By the Christmas of 1957, the exchange had moved to a new building on Oakland Avenue with all the charisma of a shoebox. Snow swirled into the old building on Pine Street, through skeletal beams where the roof used to be; it fell straight into the basement, because the floors were gone. Men of means chase the most modern thing. There'd been an earlier exchange building, erected in 1836. St. Louis had the oldest commodity trading exchange in the U.S. By the early '90s, the building on Oakland Avenue was blighted, taken by eminent domain to expand the Saint Louis Science Center. The Exchange was dissolved in 1998. And the only trace of all that money, all that power, all that grandness, is the endless back and forth of railcars crossing the Merchants Bridge.

17.

Hyde Park Beer is the beer of your fathers and Peach is the snuff of your mothers. Your people are nighttime people and springtime people, pickled egg people. Dogwoods make them sad but they don't care why. Your people came from people who frequented saloons catering to roustabouts and riverfront bums. People partial to pig knuckles and nickel whiskey. People hiding in dark bars as records drop and cigarettes glow. People in church still drunk from the night before. Sweaty people. Yelling people. People who pick up snakes with their bare hands in the name of the Father, the Son and the Holy Ghost. People who know all the words to that one song. People who name their dogs Emphysema or Son of a Bitch. Honest people. Rude people. People who go on and on. People who do anything for their people. People who aim toward moving objects. People who ask who do you think you are? Not: how are you? Or: What do you think about that? People who don't sleep much. People who don't need you. People who wrap your birthday present in the bag it came in. People who fret. People who war. People of the dog. People of the starling. Stompers of brown recluses. People who farm and name their son Virgil but never read the Georgics. People who get mad at their people who read the Georgics. People who swear. People with habits. People with horses. People who lose. People who don't close bathroom doors to pee. People who close bathroom doors to weep. People with a pig tattooed on one foot and a rooster on the other. People who never drown at sea.

18.
You think Granite City is named after the rock, but it's named after those midnight-blue enamel pans that look like a starry sky. The industry calls it graniteware but regular people call it granny speckled. The town was founded around steel mills that turned out pots and pans and big blue enamel soup spoons. The people who worked in the factories were from Armenia, Hungary, Romania, Bulgaria, Macedonia, Croatia, Mexico, and Russia. They lived around mills in a neighborhood that the map called Lincoln Place but if you asked how to get there people said Hungry Hollow is that way. In the 1950s the steel mills were so big they looked like another city, one that was always on fire. In winter, it snowed snow, and it snowed ashes. In spring and summer and fall, it snowed ashes. In the 1950s, real estate investors chartered buses to Hungry Hollow to pick up housewives. They took them to subdivisions with names like *Paddock Woods*. Paddock Woods, which wasn't in the woods. Paddock Woods, where there were no horses. Fairytales take place in the woods. Fairytales have horses. Princes ride horses. The woods are full of sunshine filtered over tree branches, wildflowers, and soft green grass. It didn't matter that these were the same houses being built in Indianapolis, Minneapolis, Metropolis, and Annapolis. You got to pick your carpets and finishes. You got a picture window that looked out over a stretch of lawn. You got a picture window had a view of a sky unclouded with ash, and air that smelled like nothing but air.

19.

It's a sepia photograph of your relatives, dancing. There's a wrestling handbill on the wall, though there are also electrical cords dangling everywhere, like the room is plugged into heaven. The girls' dance steps look simple: swing, shuffle, the jive. They're wearing striped socks and sandals, relishing how well those slick leather soles glide over linoleum during a chassé. The band is playing jazz, the deep blur of the tuba providing the bass line. Duke Ellington once said he played American music, not jazz, and in 1941, his music was all over the radio, along with news of the war. The war reorganized the bandwidths. On AM, the DJs played Jo Stafford and Perry Como and baseball games. FM played Baroque music and public service announcements. After the war, Lou Thesz, son of a shoemaker but never a heel, channeled the teachings of his Austro-Hungarian father, throwing opponents to the mat in his signature Greco-Roman wrestling style. In ancient Greece, Leontiskos of Messene won matches not by strength or speed, but his *superior finger-bending skills*. Milo of Croton, another champion, died showing off his strength by tearing a tree up by its roots. He got his hands stuck in a cleft of the trunk, and a pack of wolves ate him. Your great-grandmother soothed her insomnia watching wrestling on TV. Her favorite was The Human Orchid, Gorgeous George. Your grandmother had a mighty big crush on big, mighty Lou: always a face, never a tweener. Baptized as Aloysius. Looked like Superman. *Tore the tails off* gimmick guys, though never George. *He was a good wrestler without that baloney,* Lou said. *Bob Hope helped him put the gimmick together. Unfortunately, a lot of fellows copied him. They're just histrionic idiots. Now this fellow the Destroyer, he runs around and screams a lot. But he can really wrestle, that's all right. The gimmick wrestlers, though, they're on the way out.* On the way out like TV. On the way out like George with his golden georgie pins. On the way out like rock 'n' roll. On the way out like Ric Flair and Richard Strauss. On the way out like Superman.

20.
On New Year's Day, a day I spent stuffing straw into a Styrofoam cooler to shelter a feral cat, a man died in a Dumpster three blocks from my house. He died in the Dumpster behind the old Falstaff Brewery Apartments. People knew about it in England because it was reported on the BBC. *America has already seen its first cold-related fatality of the year, as a homeless man in St. Louis has frozen to death in a bin.* He thought getting out of the wind would help. That the insulating power of plastic trash bags would help. He was 53. Right before Christmas, a man froze to death downtown in a Port-o-Potty. He lived in it, after the city shut down New Life Evangelistic Center and opened a shelter in the old Biddle Market with 98 beds. When people couldn't get in they just walked around all night. The night time temperature in St. Louis between December 2017 and January 2018 hovered around minus 6 degrees. The police removed his belongings: *shoes, umbrella, bottle of orange juice, empty beer can, jacket, $25 Panera gift card, plastic spoon, and a debit card bearing the name Grover Perry.* He was 56 years old. At the foot of the Port-o-Potty, someone left a poinsettia, the kind you get at the drugstore with petals edged in red glitter. On every block in my neighborhood, three or four orange cats shelter under cars, or in empty buildings. My neighbor M. calls the empty house on Knapp *the cat factory.* Terry Midnight squatted in a little building on the other side of Florissant and every day fed orange cats, more than 20. They still don't know who shot him but the day he died his daughter came and spray-painted RIP DAD/SHINE BRIGHT on the front of the

building and leaned on the building and wept. Every day, people came and added something. Midnight's photo in a silver frame. Silver balloons tied to the railing, sunflowers in juice jars, grocery store roses, candles. People sat in chairs in front of the building for hours in the cold. *If I were mayor, I'd make sure every bullet was made out of rare silver and cost $10,000.* The grief became a silver music and rose like notes. It rose like notes made from smoke and silver roses and glittering light, a hymn for Terry Midnight. J. feeds Midnight's cats and P. feeds Midnight's cats and the guy who drives the mobile dental clinic feeds Midnight's cats. The cats have so much food the raccoons come out at night and eat the leftovers. *An address is just an address, how does it magically make you a human being?* My neighbor who sees ghosts said the dead don't go anywhere. Right now there's a lady here named Fran who grew sweet potatoes in her garden, she said. An older guy with a limp, he says his name is George, she said. He's friendly, he says he's a protector. So many ghosts, she said. They're sad about the falling-down buildings and they're sad about us falling down too. The dead grieve, she said, just like the living. A whole choir of mourners, visible and invisible, heartbroken together.

21.
Blessed are the pie-bakers of Chicago, the women *who begin work at 3 o'clock in the afternoon and continue until about 2 o'clock the next morning,* the women with one good coat and two pairs of passable shoes and two bad eyes *who make the crust of the pie and put it in the pan,* who, *like a morning paper compositor, sleep in the day time.* Blessed are the girls who pack crackers and ginger snaps. Blessed are the girls who pack cans of baking soda in well-lit factories. Blessed are the gummers and folders of envelopes, the inspectors of horseshoe nails, the scrap-paper sorters singing *brilla, brilla, la stallina.* Blessed are the morning paper compositors, drawing down the roman shades. Blessed are the women and girls of the rattan-works, bottoming chairs. Blessed are the girls who pack tobacco, the stenographers and clerks, the sewers of muslin underwear. Blessed are the stitchers of patches and regalia, attachers of military fringe, braiders of silver cord. Blessed are the painters of silk banners, the painters of all-seeing eyes on Odd Fellows flags. Blessed are the makers of cuffs and ties, the affixers of buttons. Blessed are the telephone operators, *the day force, the extra force, the night force, the relief force.* Blessed are the head milliners and the telegraph operators, the canners of tapioca, the insulators of silk-wrapped wires. Blessed are the box-makers, the sorters and the trimmers. Blessed are the turners, the vampers, the eyeleters. Blessed are the women of Blue Island, the women of Throop, the women of Ashland and Gault and Noble. Blessed are the girls of North Division and the girls of South Division. Blessed are the finishers. Blessed are the closers. Blessed are the stayers.

22.

Ages ago, during a winter back when it snowed when it was supposed to snow, and the temperature rose and fell in predictable and elegant ways, a kid in footie pajamas sat on a heat register, staring into the darkness of the living room. He could see a giant something behind the tree, wrapped in yards of red foil paper, Bubble-Lites shimmering over its surface. He knew what it was. For one thing, it was so damn big! And months before, his mother sat at the kitchen table with a fountain pen and a cup of black coffee, the Sears Wish Book marked up, inky blue circles drawn around floating hands wearing suede gloves, or a disembodied foot in a shearling house slipper. And (and!) she'd circled some sleds: the Flexible Flyer, the Flying Arrow, and best of all, the plastic-topped Silver Comet. Yeah, an inner tube would do you. One kid's dad nailed sheet metal to the bottom of a wooden box. Another kid's brother fumbled wooden pallets together into something that looked like a giant, deformed catfish skeleton on runners. It flew down snowy hills, but when it tumbled, it threatened to gash open a hand or an eyeball. The runners had strips of soda can nailed on. And it gave you slivers through your mittens. Better the brand name, the curly script, the steel runners, the sturdiness of industrial assembly. Of course, he'd never want to replace actual snow with that white angel hair his mother swathed the Nativity set in. It gave him glass slivers. But like his mom, he preferred machine-made. Not earth tones, but primary colors. Not his grandmother's lumpy brown scarves or mittens with weird colored stripes, but the perfect machine-knitted acrylic ones in snowflake patters. And on cars, on tools, and especially on sleds, he loved that perfectly placed factory rivet no barehanded human could ever remove.

37

23.
The fifth of July is a holiday but no one will admit it. That's the day I walk through the neighborhood, sidewalks covered with singed, starry paper. The asphalt of the middle school is covered with deflated fire cones and bent sparkler wires. The empty shells of paper tanks. The empty casings of Knock-Outs, Screamers, Majestic Brocades. On the fourth of July I sat on the roof and watched fountains of fire strobing through the darkness, sparkling off the metal skin of the Arch. Seventy years ago, they tore down a neighborhood to build the Arch. They tore down the type foundries. The bohemian bars. The cold-water flats. St. Joseph's School. The Old Rock House, where Mark Twain's great-uncle sold waxed sails and tack, and where Rockhouse Annie sang. Where W.H. Handy came to listen to her, where he sat in his wheelchair, nursing a bourbon, remembering his slumber on the rocks of the levee, and the woman who cried about her lover's heart, a rock thrown into the sea. I sat on my roof watching the shadows thrown under shots of gold brocades and silver chrysanthemums. Rockets, artillery shells, smoke balls. Hiss of a match. White dotted line in the sky. Last year, on Bastille Day, Mark Twain's uncle's mansion burned. James Clemens, who built a house that was really a sarcophagus for his dead wife, her face carved into every lintel and all the moldings. She died of the cholera. Flames 100 feet in the air, every fireman in the city there. Her name was Eliza. They called it the Valentine's Mansion and then they called it the Clemens Mansion. Nuns lived there. Nuns handed out peanut-and-jelly sandwiches and cartons of

milk to anyone who walked through the door. When
the Clemons House burned it rained Rorschach shapes,
black chunks of chrysolite, jagged asbestos scattered
across every lawn. The Clemens Mansion is gone and
now it's field covered in straw, tiny green shoots sprouting
through ash and rubble. Since childhood, I have
dreamed about Pompeii. That I was there. On Bastille
Day fire was falling from the sky, pieces of old wood on
fire flying down the street, carried by hot wind. Birds
whirl in the evening sky like falling sparks. A tall boy
at the bus stop bisects a peach with the spine of a black
comb. Someone's grandpa drags his oxygen tank into
the gas station, singing with the radio, *something's
always there to remind me.* Let's count all these losses
like rocks at the bottom of the sea. Let's count these losses
like rocks at the bottom of the Mississippi. Let's put a
match to the sky-lanterns, light the repeaters, the artillery
shell filled with intractable stars. Let's bust out the
pneumatics, the hylectics, let's conjure aeonial beings.
Let's become bright pieces of fire, shining. Let's become
sparks of pneuma, falling through the dark sky of July.
So damned pretty.

24.

Greyhound's Streamline Moderne buses weren't any faster, but the curves and racing stripes suggested they might be part rocket ship. They rolled into matching terminals with curvilinear walls and porthole windows. The New Madrid halfway station, smack dab between St. Louis and Memphis, had a coffee counter, though traveling salesmen and farmers still stuck near the steps, smoking hand-rolled cigarettes and drinking coffee from Thermoses. In early spring, 1938, László Bíró patented the ballpoint pen, which is why the French call them *biros*. Superman debuted in *Action Comics No. 1*, and the *Aviazione Legionaria,* under Franco's orders, showered Alicante with bombs. Just as the first steamship on the Mississippi was thought to portend the New Madrid earthquake of 1811, a fashionable new bus depot selling cheap tickets could augur disaster for a small town. The river didn't run backwards; houses didn't fall; green lightning didn't flash out of fissures in the earth. But young men and women donned Army uniforms or sweater suits and packed their pasteboard suitcases. They stood on the chrome bus stairs, waving goodbye, echoing the words of those superstitious farmers who watched the river change its course and cried, *If we do not get away from here, the ground is going to eat us alive.*

25.
In the morning, they resurfaced the rink, buffed it with water until it was slick and clear and you could see into the interior of the ice, even with cloudy patches here and there, like flocked Christmas windows. You tried to skate your name in cursive, wobbling as the blade refused to accommodate the curvy loops of B's or lowercase L's. And then you fell down. You would pause, pretending to be stunned, staring into the ice for just a moment. You knew there was something down there. You imagined it was silver coins, and white doilies, and a howling lumberjack with his pet bear, frozen and suspended. If you didn't get up fast enough, your gloves would stick to the ice, just a little. Later, in the afternoon, when the ice was scarred and opaque, you would give up looking for anything. You would skate to the far edge of the rink and sit on a bench by a fire, and drink hot chocolate out of someone else's dad's Thermos, and talk to kids who didn't go to your school, who you would never see again. And in the thin air, the sound of Johnny Cash playing on someone's car radio; someone smoking in their Plymouth, the windows rolled down, though it was cold. This was when moths still liked to chew on your mother's scarves and sweaters. When anchormen's hair fell below their collars, and dads didn't feel embarrassed to wear fur coats with a hood, and dogs could go more places than they couldn't. When the girls on the playground all wanted to be the same ice ballerina, and it was easily pretended, with white skates and wool coats and knit gloves decorated with pixelated flowers.

26.

They call it fanning. The yellowing of leaves on one branch at the crown. It means the tree is doomed. That under its bark, beetles are chewing swoopy hieroglyphs in the wood, infecting the tree with fungus. When you peel back the bark it looks like the bugs have been hard at work drawing shapes and having a little art show, so they call it a *beetle gallery*. In the late 1950s, no one noticed it. No one looked for beetles. No one noticed it till 1961, a drought year, when all the elms began to die. Eight years later, the Cuyahoga caught on fire. Nine years later, astronauts turned the camera around so we could look at ourselves from outer space. Mothers and fathers watched astronauts bounce on the moon through cat-eyed and horn-rimmed glasses. They felt like crying but they didn't cry. They developed mysterious headaches and stomachaches. They visited cemeteries and dug holes on Arbor Day and forgot to plant the tree. They stopped eating things out of boxes. Fathers abandoned their bowling leagues for re-enacting, smoking Meerschaum pipes, growing their whiskers, asking their wives to make them simple linen shirts and linen pants. Fathers left on camping trips with their friends but left their tents and fishing poles at home, pretended to be blacksmiths and ropemakers and rugmakers, played *bouillotte* with hand-painted cards. Fathers wore funny little caps and joined drum and bugle corps. They forged their own swords in the garage. Mothers threw out their girdles and daytime gloves and rat-tailed combs. Ran their unpolished nails down the columns of university catalogs.

Wore tiger suits on Halloween. Waited till everyone was asleep and planted pin oaks, sweet gums, thornless locust, white burch, and tulip trees in the dark yard. Dialed up the blazing phone tree on rotary. Forgot the rosary. Opened candle shops. Opened ceramics shops. Learned guitar. Taught guitar. Opened guitar shops. Refused to brew the coffee during social hour at church. Refused to sew simple linen shirts and linen pants for their husbands. Kissed the neighbor behind a tree during a neighborhood parade. Said I remember climbing elms, hand over hand, foot by foot. The city says it cut them down when they got sick but I say they were never there at all. A figment of a figment. Something fractured. A fragment. We remember a tunnel of green trees and really all along the streets were bare. Those elms we remember were never really there. We imagined them. The girl who climbed the tree was never there. The girl I thought I was: she was never there. The one who put crackers and butter and caramels and comic books in a pillowcase and climbed a tree was never there. The one who climbed the tree, who sat in the upper canopy and said, hey tree, you have a crown and I have a crown. We are the queens, the queens of every one, every body, every thing.

27.

Fabric stores, running your hand on the glossy rectangles
stapled with buttons, yellow, white, pink. Spools of thread,
shining like blue and green hair. Your mother at the Singer,
sewing dresses. Back in school, sitting next to the seeth-
ing steam radiator, you fold your hands on your desktop.
It's one of the first days of school in your new itchy
sweater, a dark spot of sweat on your chest, like your heart
is leaking condensation. All the way down the hall, loafers
squeaking, you imagine a thought bubble over each foot
like in the comics, imagining just what your shoes could be
complaining about today. One night your mother cooks a
chicken; you and your sister pull the wishbone apart.
You get the big half. You wish you were a clever princess,
a pirate, a girl in a book, frozen and graceful like the
mermaids in the fountain, anything to get away from the
bore of the day, the burrs in socks, soaping off the plates
and the water glasses, handing them to your sister to dip
in the rinse water. In September, the night falls faster and
faster and the crickets get quieter every night, and there's a
choky, weird sadness that you don't know how to describe.
It feels like a premonition, you older, drinking coffee,
reading newspapers, cooking, steam coming off a pan of
boiling water in the early evening. And kids, slamming the
screen door hard. The ring of a telephone, not the wrong
number but the wrong receiver, a lady looking for some-
one who is not you. You will take your hand and rip the
phone cord right out of the wall, you will grab the artery
filled with dull, sparking witchery and you will put a stop
to it, you will pull it out by the roots, you will evoke the

name of Jesus. It is a terrible but divine electrocution, a moment of devastation, realizing how love and grace hide in the gray containers of the dull day-to-day, the making of lunches, the over-and-over of *Happy Birthday to You*. You wash your face in the kitchen sink. You walk out the door to the neighbor's house and ask to use the phone. It's an emergency. You have to call your sister.

28.
Barn swallows don't need barns. They'll dart through any broken pane. Ants aren't discerning. They'll venture into a mostly empty can of malt liquor, or happily eat stale French fries tossed out a car window. And when there's no maintenance guy to puff weedkiller on the lawn, it recedes to a calendar of plants we call weeds that are really plants. That calendar begins in March with henbit, and then cycles through clover, dandelions, chicory, plantain, amaranth, crab grass, spurge, joint grass. In the summer of 1968, the roads and highways of America were dotted with hitch-hiking kids, some so dirty, they seemed like God's original dust poppets. Surely some sought out cryptoforests for a midday snooze under the cover of a floppy leather hat, or leaned on a busted-up cinderblock wall reading J.R.R. Tolkien, temporary king of a postindustrial Middle Earth. Maybe one stopped to sit on the front steps of the abandoned power house on 18th Street, pulled a smoke out of his patch pocket, and fiddled with his transistor, searching for the sonic-boom bass line of Cream's *Sunshine of Your Love,* the radio's antenna telescoped as if scanning the sky for a flying saucer. Maybe he made contact. Maybe the alien telegraphed an answer. If so, it never reached the power station. The city tore it down in 1987, though the foundation remains, along with the 196-foot-tall smoke-stack. Its replacement is on the same footprint. It looks very '80s, with pink-orange brick and green metal awnings. Now, it's where the so-called alternative station's broadcast tower beams out the flavor of the month, the grubby drug anthems replaced with serotonin-reuptake banjo riffs.
A temporary mystery forest filled with crows and trees and carpenter bees. Real estate waiting to happen.

29.
Ice sings when it melts and freezes and shifts. The idea sounds cute, but if you've heard it, you know the sound is occult and sinister, like a steel cable being stretched, or the whining of lasers, or extraterrestrial signals creaking through the chilly darkness of space. Once a decade, the Mississippi River freezes completely—it's called an "ice gorge"—and people cross it from the Missouri side or the Illinois side, headed for the opposite bank. They've gone on foot, on skates and bicycles, pushing baby carriages, driving mule-drawn wagons or Buicks, just because they could. The newspapers always warn people away, printing histrionic quotes from finger-wagging city fathers and dour engineers about "air holes" waiting to suck down some dumb Joe, whose last look at Earth would be through the distorted transparency of an ice sheet. But go out as dusk is falling and look towards the Eads Bridge, and you may see an endless line of people in their dark winter clothes marching across, like a stream of determined ants headed for a bread crust. The ice is there to walk on; they must go. And anyway, dumb Joes are Joes without instincts. Any barge worker, any farmer, any skunked working stiff taking a shortcut across the river at 4 a.m. after a night at some shady bar on the opposite shore knows to bring a long stick to test the ice. They know when the *zeeeeppps* and *squuurrrrrrrrs* grow loud and acute, the ice is moving, and you walk another direction. They know the river doesn't want to eat them alive. And though its voice is bleak and metallic, it doesn't lie; you just have to stop and listen, and it will always give you the right directions for home.

30.
Back in the day, it was easy for the son of a Prussian shepherd to make it big in the drug business. The business pages referred to him as C.F.G. Meyer, short for Christian Frederick Gottlieb, but everyone called him Fred. He sold his flock and came to America with 12 Prussian dollars in his pocket. He moved to Indiana and piloted a canal boat in Fort Wayne. One day, a man on the dock said to him, *Here, bub, do you want a job?* Fred nodded and the man took him to a drugstore, and told them *here is a boy who wants something to do.* Fred built the fire. Fred washed bottles. From time to time Fred *pulverized gum aloes, euphorbium, cantharides and similar articles.* Fred and his brother Bill pooled their dollars. Fred and his brother moved to St. Louis. Fred and Bill filed with the State of Missouri as *Meyer & Brother,* purveyors of mortars and pestles, sellers of Balsam of Peru, Elatarium, and Alum. Sellers of label-under-glass bottles and crutch tips. Fred and Bill were killing it. Fred and Bill manufactured bottled drugs and Soul Kiss perfume. The brothers sold drugs but also valentines, gumdrops, lipsticks and julep straws. Bill and Fred invented the drugstore soda fountain. Fred built a mansion on Keokuk Street. Fred's son Henry nearly destroyed the empire, returning from South Africa with 500 veterans of the Boer Wars, paying them out of the family fortune to relive their battles on the 1904 World's Fair grounds. Close to Fred's heart were his symbolic sons, the company sons. Close to Fred's heart was Irish John from Chicago. Irish John who sold Meyers' drugs while making saccharin in his bathtub.

Irish John who sold saccharin on the cheap and destroyed Germany's monopoly. Irish John who invested in property along the North Riverfront. Irish John who founded a company named for his wife, Olga Mendez Monsanto. Irish John who undertook the manufacture of caffeine and aspirin. Fred's warehouses stood packed full of John's saccharine and aspirin. John and all the salesmen gathered on Keokuk one Christmas Eve to give Fred a *grandfather's clock*. Fred at 72, thin-faced, wearing his pince-nez. Seated in his study, surrounded by his sons. The flames in the fireplace throwing shadows on the faces of men with their glossy hair and their whiskers. Shadows on the hides of zebras, springboks, and bears Henry shot in Johannesburg. The smell of pine pitch, the snapping of the fire. A mantle merry with holly and white tapers, but the feeling of death, of something pale and terminal, something invisible present. The vapors from good scotch dissolving into dry air, the convulsing smoke from pipes and cigars rising in the air like so much ectoplasm at a séance, like so much saccharin dissolving into coffee.

31.

Walt Whitman wrote poems about bridges, trains, and telegraph lines in tribute to his favorite brother, Jeff. His brother Jeff was in charge of all of our water, and all of our pipes. Jeff didn't build the Bissell Street Tower, like Walt bragged he did, but he kept the water clean, and when the water wasn't clean he told everyone to drink beer so they wouldn't get sick from the cholera. Jeff knew James Eads, the famous bridge builder, and Henry Flad, the engineer from Baden, whose name graces a street sign here that everyone snickers at because it sounds funny, because the average Joe doesn't know of the great Henry Flad. Jeff wrote to his mother after his wife Mattie died, or *Dearest Matty* as Walt called her, *beloved Matty— I took my horse and buggy arriving at the house abt 3ck—I found Mattie dressed—furs &c on—sitting awaiting me—I took her in my arms and carried her out to the buggy as I sat her in—she said "wait now 'till I fix my dress"—these were the last words she spok—She then fell over on her side I immediately took her back to the room and sat her in the chair—she knew me yet—but could not speak...* Jeff moved to Pine Street with his little girls, Jessie and Hattie, short for Mannahatta, after her uncle's famous poem. Jeff wrote to Walt, begged him to visit, but Walt lay in bed, paralyzed by grief and a stroke. When Walt came to St. Louis, he walked to Mr. Ead's bridge every morning. He sat on the shore of the river, staring at the bridge for hours, contemplating its cantilevers and its caissons sunk down so deep they touched the fossils of trilobites. He toured all the kindergartens, where all the kids thought he was Santa Claus, and he just smiled and nodded. He walked and thought to stay but knew he would leave. He wrote his sister Lou that *there are just two things here you & I w'd never get used to, & would spoil all—that is the air you breathe is always tainted with coal smoke & pungent gas—& a perpetual dust & smut & little black motes, that forever smut your clothes & hands & face, all the time, night & day—So you see there are always some bad points, even to the greatest & best—But the folks here don't seem to mind it, or think it is any thing.*

32.
Madam Z., Mr. Z's wife, read cards and palms at the Egyptian Tea Room. We went to the Egyptian Tea Room one cold night, a little after Christmas. I wore my new coat, my good coat, green and turquoise, shiny like a peacock's body. I put on pink lipstick and little pearl earrings. I drank Turkish coffee, which seemed like a strange thing to drink at the Egyptian Tea Room. I went into the back room, through a doorway shrouded in beads and silver fabric, to get my fortune told. She turned over the cards and said, *how strange, you see? All 8s.* Eight like the lemiscate over the head of the Magician and the woman on the Strength card and the man at the edge of the seasick ocean, juggling two pentacles. Eight like the devil. Eight like the world. Saturn's eights. That was the night the cops showed up. That was the night they broke the front glass door with their clubs and their boots and arrested us all, slapped cuffs on us for violating Section 625 of the Revised Code of 1914, the anti-soothsaying law. *How biblical can you get? Can a modern cop suffer a witch to live? Can a lady get a light around here? How can a lady get her bail met?* Mrs. Z. came on WIL every week, took callers and pulled cards. She was on the air every week between Louie's Hungry Five and the Palais d'Or Orchestra. She got bags and bags of fan mail. Mrs. Z. was in plain sight. Where were the cops? Why didn't they bust her on the radio? Now Mrs. Z is in jail and the café is closed forever and all the debutantes carry on with their Fortune Teas at the St. Louis Women's Club,

casting horoscopes and reading palms and dressing in black velvet and head wraps and big gold necklaces and big gold earrings. The paper runs recipes for orange fortune cakes, like a fortune cookie but not as dry and crumbly and with a lot more icing. They run recipes for the ladies who throw teas and pull cards and trace the lines on palms and say you're going to love that one, marry that one, break this other one's heart. It's OK for the fortunate to tell fortunes, for those who always get their say to soothsay. Me and the people I know, we shut our mouth and pose for the mugshot. Smoke and smoke and drink hope like a liquor, never able to stop putting our hearts on cards and palms and horses. We say we think those things in sky called stars are really bullet holes. We say Bingo is our name-o. We say that's just the way it is when you are born under a burned-out star. We say that's just the breaks. That's just what happens when you're born a crazy eight.

33.
An old-timey livery stable seems so wholesome. But often, right next to the stable, there'd be a saloon. That proximity definitely caused some situations, like the night that Morris Gahan and Charles Noye, stablehands at Kramer's Livery and Undertaking, drank a lot of whiskey, went back to the barn, and quarreled. Noye shot his friend in the mouth with a .45 pistol. Gahan's giant, white teeth, *nearly as strong as those of a horse,* stopped the bullet. He fell down; he got up. He spat out the lead bullet, three teeth, some blood, and took a nap in the hay. *I felt no pain, and I didn't know I had lost my teeth until I heard them rattle on the stable floor,* he said. *I picked them up with the bullet, and will keep them as souvenirs.* Suicides gravitated to the stables, and bombers— including one maladroit who constructed *a regular Chicago anarchist's bomb* from dynamite, bullets, sand, sawdust, and a defective fuse. Weird things happened in liveries. There was a horse, tickled under the chin, which laughed itself to death; a stablehand who coughed so hard he gave himself a hemorrhage; and a little mustang named Nuts, who memorized the address of 111 boarding horses, and led them home unaccompanied. If teeth rattled on the stable floor, so did dice, and there were always horse thieves around, like James McGann, also known as the man who had a fight with a bass viol during a midnight burglary. After *his fingers swept across the strings of the bass fiddle, evoking a Wagnerian crash of music,* he turned, punched the instrument, and was arrested escaping with it. A more clever fellow washed Butcher Maybrie's coal-colored pony

in peroxide, disguising him as a sorrel—but the horse's curly coat gave him away. *Mr. Maybrie says he will not attempt to keep his horse's hair light*, the paper explained. *Blondine costs too much by the barrel. And besides— he prefers the natural black.*

34.

A long time ago, Famous-Barr kept artists on its payroll, people who built tiny castles and sleighs and elves for Christmas windows. That was back when Famous-Barr had a fancy restaurant on the top floor and sold secret recipe onion soup and hosted renowned musicians from all over the planet. One October, they brought in Mrs. Ethel Romelfanger (formerly Judevine; née Luckey), official organist at the Circus World Museum in Baraboo. Mrs. Romelfanger played air calliope, flanked by shaker chimes and a Unafone, at the Beautiful American Festival. She wore a metallic tunic and wooden high-heeled sandals. She played hits off her 1961 record, *American Steam Calliope Concert II:* "Camptown Races," "Sweet Georgia Brown" and "Happy Birthday." She finished with cuts off her recent self-titled album, including covers of "Love Child" and "Magic Carpet Ride." Billboard's Circus Trouping column gave that record four stars, she told us. It ran next to ads for actual circus work. Cole Bros. sought a winter-season fortuneteller; Buckeye Circus needed a menagerie man to drive a hitch with white mules; Rudy Bros. announced it wanted a second Elephant Man. Ethel coughed. Not that kind. He means a day laborer, she said, a guy who works with elephants, a reliable and sober guy who can drive a truck. Ethel told us it was harder and harder to run away and join the circus. She said this as a faithful reader of *Billboard's* Final Curtain section, which ran death notices of notable circus folk, including Tito Flint the clown; George Lake of Lake Bros. Penny Arcades; and Kelly the Candy Man, veteran concessionaire. She told us she played even the happy songs like funeral hymns these days. She tried to play a funeral hymn for the circus itself, but if you did it proper there'd be a brass band plaing Karl King songs, and a choir of clowns without makeup, and a secret showperson's version of "Abide With Me," with lyrics about stomped-on cotton candy under the bleachers after the lights go down, and trains rolling on to the next town forevermore, accompanied by a wistful bearded lady playing the harmonica, playing that harp with all the sadness of ages, like she was trying to play those notes in the same pitch as cold rain falling outside tent flaps on the last day of the last circus ever.

35.

Back then the sky turned a different color, more turquoise, not that faded-out color you see today, the old people say. That's why you saw turquoise everywhere, that's why they used it for plastic ashtrays and the seats inside a Crown Victoria Skyliner. You think that's turquoise. No. That's sky blue. Back then red was not just red, but eyes-squeezed-shut, blood-vessels-popping, Norwegian poppy red, the color of stewardesses' lipstick and the color of bear tongues, like in the Polaroids that happy campers took as grizzlies ate trash and licked their chops in Yellowstone Park. Back then the color gold was so bright it left tracers and auras in your eyes, made you feel like you'd poked yourself in the eye. The air always smelled like spearmint chewing gum. Or fancy *eau de toilette*. No one wears *eau de toilette* anymore, they say. Cause no one even can spell that, much less understand what it is. Back then no one weighed more than 140 pounds. Back then, no one wore dirty shoes with strings coming off them. Did we smoke 'em if we had 'em? Yeah, we smoked 'em if we had 'em. Cigarettes didn't cause cancer back then. Maybe you got rickets or pertussis or beriberi, that's all. And when you took the train, sitting in your grandmother's lap or your grandfather's lap, a box of chicken and a Thermos full of coffee on the seat beside you, outside the big windows, the whole world was blue and red and green and gold and perfect. The whole world, a zoetrope.

36.

All that blue pouring from the windows, as if the sky itself had decided to move in and set up house. A mansion made of yellow bricks that almost looked like gold bars. The railroad baron built it, a wedding present for his son Z. and Mary, his bride. Mary, whose father invented the cigarette that James Bond would smoke one day. Mary, whose money came from cigarettes the Great Gatsby would smoke someday. The same cigarette Jean Seberg would smoke at the end of *Breathless* one day. Seven years after their wedding, the police found Z. walking the streets of St. Louis, sobbing and shouting at the sky. The court *adjudged him insane,* and sent him to the sanitarium. Mary would send her next four husbands there, too. The papers only say the court found Z. insane. No one says what sanitarium. Perhaps the state asylum, an *eleemosynary institution,* a place where, as a former 3rd Ward alderman noted, the food was worse than *door hinges and gravy, with a side order of rusty nails.* Or maybe to the Widow Rethwilm's, also known as The House of Mystery, *a big stone mansion with a well-kept lawn, standing among spreading shade trees in one of St. Louis' most fashionable neighborhoods.* The widow treated the mad and the gravely ill with the Kneipp cure, with ice baths and sitz baths and saltless *kneippbrød.* She hid her charges from her fashionable neighbors for years. She hid it till the Health Commissioner showed up after getting complaints of bellowing and shrieking issuing from her gracious residence. They showed up and Mrs. Rethwilm told them it was her naughty parrot. Then the neighbors saw *men often appearing on the lawn, especially in the morning, bare-footed and otherwise in costumes rather negligé.* They spied men and women, their skirts lifted and trousers rolled, sawing wood in the backyard. They saw, in the middle of the night, an undertaker's carriage, carrying bodies away. Four suicides, *an advanced case of the dropsy,* a heart attack, *a case of brain shock,* one case of yellow jaundice. I fed them bread, said the widow, and did not charge them. Hard work is part of the cure, said the widow. Not that I'm a doctor, said the widow. I merely *operate a philanthropic health institution. Friends came to me for treatment. Strangers began coming. I couldn't turn them away.* Strangers like the young man in a fine suit and a long beard and silvery eyes. A young man with eyes like nickel slugs. A bitter groom. A wretched boy with a wrecked mind and a wrecked heart. A man who came to the table to eat free bread with all the other wrecked men, raking his fingers through his long tangled hair and long tangled beard, singing, over and over, *I'm combing out my grief, I'm combing out my grief.*

37.
The International Ladies' Garment Workers' Union threw a Christmas party for their kids. One woman played a lopsided piano in the corner, and the cast crept out from behind a folding screen: a black cat, a fairy with a feather duster, elves and more elves. These seamstresses were among the 200 who struck against Forest City Manufacturing in 1935, when the company itself was astonished by its profits during the Depression. *It was a simple process,* wrote the *St. Louis Labor Advocate. Pay low wages and sell at high prices; see?* Now, the sickly electricity of war crackled everywhere, the color of dulled lead tinsel. Roosevelt gave ominous speeches about swords and plowshares, and King George read poems on the radio: *I said to the man who stood at the gate of the year, give me a light that I may tread safely into the unknown.* And a skinny girl at the Christmas party, no costume but her pointe shoes, danced across the bare wood floor. She chucked The *Nutcracker* to dance what she felt, like a shamaness trying to banish a typhoon.

38.
When your grandmother visited from California she washed her rayon dresses and pantyhose in the bathtub, swirling them in lukewarm water sudsy with a special soap she bought from Avon. At night she had a chiffon bonnet she wrapped around her hair and it looked like a green pastel halo when she knelt by her little bed to pray. Your grandmother grew up in a big house with a ballroom that's filled with wasp nests now. The French doors to the ballroom cracked in 1983. Your grandmother's mother's mother was French. Your grandmother played in the bell choir and ran committees at church. She gave you hotel room Bibles and cellophane tape for Christmas. Your grandmother took you and your sisters and aunties and cousins to a tea at the Sheraton-Jefferson Gold Room to see a historical fashion show to raise money for the ladies' bell choir at church. Your grandmother subscribed to *The Upper Room* magazine. She memorized scripture. The aunties on the other side of the family checked out books from the library like Betty Friedan's *The Feminine Mystique* and Helen Gurley Brown's *Sex and the Single Girl,* written on Helen's famous silver typewriter. The middle-aged women at the fashion show smiled and tried to look delighted but their faces betrayed a hint of Puritan disapproval and *tristesse*. The tabletops were cluttered with coffee cups, Coke bottles, empty dessert plates and dirty ashtrays. Back then a lady never left home without a brooch or sprayed hair, but there was a point when you were expected to embrace the gravitas of wrinkles and a bearish figure. Helen Gurley Brown wore miniskirts and fishnets until she was 80. She wrote a telegram on her silver

typewriter telling the words *ma'am, matron*, and *dowager* to go to hell. She survived on saccharin and caffeine and the words she wrote on her silver typewriter. Your grandmother taught typing at a high school. In high school you sat in the backseat of your father's station wagon listening to your grandmother say she'd go to dinner but she'd just sit with us and have a coffee with a little bit of Sweet'n Low. In high school it seemed impossible that there would be a day when you would stop wearing silver dresses. That you would stop wanting to see your own face in the mirror in the morning. That one day, you'd refuse to eat cake for breakfast. That one day you would feel ashamed to fold silver paper airplanes written with love notes to launch in the air toward your crush. That one day you'd have coffee for breakfast or dinner. That the day would come when you'd stop watching for silver sails all out of the west under the silver moon.

39.
If the '70s had never happened, stores wouldn't have to put *shirt and shoes* required stickers in their front windows. It was the era of the guy with long wavy hair and long wavy mustache; the guy in thongs with rainbow soles; the guy who, when he ran out of smokes, ambled to the store wearing nothing but cutoffs and a tan. The same guy who gave us the disco-era roller rink, after slyly noticing the availability of skateboard-style plastic wheels. With no more skate keys, no more metal wheels, no more feeling like your teeth were vibrating like tiny Tesla coils, everyone wanted to skate. The smoking men with wavy hair aimed to deliver that experience to all, though their establishments weren't entirely wholesome. There were arcade games, and the guy in the DJ booth played *The Hokey Pokey* but he also played *Do You Think I'm Sexy?* and *Le Freak*. The lights were turned low; disco lights blittered on the walls. There was a mirror ball in the middle of the skating floor, and a smoke machine.
On Saturday afternoons, little girls showed up in Fireball skates with pom-pom laces and satiny jackets with a chubby tube of Bonne Bell lip gloss stuck in the pocket, but they knew to stay off the floor when the DJ queued up *Another One Bites the Dust,* because it made the high-school boys skate fast and backward. *Babe* brought out the teenage couples who'd whirr around, one hand stuck in the other's back jeans pocket (the one without the giant plastic comb sticking out), and knock a kid down, or into a cinderblock wall, without an apology. When the little girls crouched down to tie their laces, they narrowed

their eyes at those dumb girls reeking of Love's Baby Soft, in their blue eye shadow and blue jeans and feathered bangs. But when a lame song came on—maybe *Owner of a Lonely Heart* by Yes—and it was safe to skate slow, they pushed out onto the floor, their faces deadpan so no one could tell what they were thinking. And that was when they dreamed of the day when they would wear *green* eye shadow, not blue, and "wheels" would no longer mean red, white, and blue Fireballs, but some guy's fast car.

40.

Pull out the wedding album and you see that people getting married in South St. Louis in 1969 looked like people from 1959. The men wore tortoiseshell glasses and close shaves and the blondes looked like brunettes, their hair was so slicked so heavily with Brylcreem. The bride wore a long skirt and long sleeves and a plain tulle veil and her attendants wore dresses that looked like novitiate jumpers. If you walked out of the picture frame and went to someone's car and turned on the radio you would expect to hear Pat Boone or Sheb Wooley singing that stupid Purple People Eater song. But this is just a couple years before a purple-haired Todd Rundgren pounded out "Hello It's Me" on *The Midnight Special,* polka-dotted feathers glued to his eyebrows. Your hip cousin went to that little cinderblock club on West Florissant called Bruno's Bat Cave and knew Gayle McCormick, who'd already moved to Los Angeles and was famous for five minutes because she sang "Baby, It's You" with a Band Called Smith. It sounded way better than the Burt Bacharach version. No one at the wedding knew A Band Called Smith. Everyone at the wedding knew Burt Bacharach. Your dad never traded the hair tonic for man bangs or feathered hair, much less eyebrows with feathers on them. He resisted the look of the times, resisted the siren call of unisex cuts and hooded jumpsuits. Your dad was the kind of dad who went to Ace's Cowshed Lounge to hear Lonesome George Kelly on the organ, but avoided the Sunday Ragtime Sing-a-long with Crazy Polly. Your hip cousin moved to California and joined

MUFON. Your hip and way-out cousin obsesses over St. Germain and his pale purple aura and bought a telescope to look for him blazing through outer space. Your hip and moonstruck cousin says there's no such thing as time, there's no such thing as space.

41.

This is the year sugar rationing ended, when mothers tossed their recipes for apple pandowdy or wartime custards flavored with Postum and honey. This is the year utility dresses gave way to Dior's New Look, with its swooshy skirts that looked like they'd been sewn from the drapes. This is the year people stopped patching shoes, darning socks, reusing bacon drippings. This is the year people planted rosebushes in their victory plots. This is the year that mothers put their kids on the Whip at the Forest Park Highlands, and went off to the picnic pavilion to smoke a cigarette. This is the year all the little boys wore dark new jeans and mothers matched little girls' hair ribbons to their dresses and ankle socks. This is the year Howdy Doody went on the air for the first time on NBC's *Puppet Playhouse.* This is the year little kids began agitating for Wonder Bread because Mr. Doody swore it was *the best bread, the kind that builds bodies eight ways.* This is the year mothers opened the door to greet Tupperware's carrot ladies, who sold the containers on the fact that burping lids preserved leftovers so much better than the plastic shower caps they'd been using. This is the year that a failed barbecue joint called McDonald's rose from the ashes after rejiggering its business plan, making hamburgers like the Ford plant made Custom Tudors. This is the year the Highlands burned down, burning so hot it buckled the asphalt on Highway 40 and sent overheated firemen to jump into the park's swimming pool. This is the year those kids on the Whip would've gone to college. This is the year those kids cried when they heard the news about the Highlands burning down. This is the year whole cities were on fire, the simple nuclear family a thing of the past, and yellow fallout-shelter signs posted over the doorways of libraries and schools. This is the year that America, eager to ditch one-egg wonder cakes and make-do-and-mend for just a bit of hope and unrationed meat and sugar, would hardly seem to have existed at all.

42.

A long time ago every big city had another little city within it, built near train tracks or industrial waterways or dumps. It was where you went after you lost your job and your house, where you patched together shelter from scrap metal, driftwood, and pallets. You nailed flattened sardine cans over holes in the floor. You curled a sheet of rusty tin into a tipsy chimney that puffed smoke over a tar-paper roof. St. Louis' ran a full mile along the Mississippi River, near the Municipal Bridge. It was so big, it spawned suburbs—Hoover Heights, Merryland, and Happyland, short for Happy Landing. Five thousand people lived there. Some of the buildings were *so big, they soared two stories tall and had antebellum verandas.* There was a scrap-metal church and an orange-crate church. People sent their kids to school, hung wash, angled for catfish and turtles, walked three blocks to the Welcome Inn, where they stood in line under the bridge for baskets of bruised turnips and stale bread. Chicago burned its Hooverville. New York sent demolition crews to Central Park. St. Louis sent a crew of WPA workers to tear down the Mississippi River shanties. In 1959, 47 families still lived in Parkerville, at the foot of Madison Street. At the foot of Madison Street, where the city of St. Louis decided to build its new municipal dock, and rallied the bulldozers. Parkerville, home to a woman who said, *This is the only home I have ever owned. I've lived here for 21 years. I'm going to miss the flowers in my garden.* Home to a man who said, *I don't want to be jammed up in one of those public housing projects. I wish I could move to the country.* Home to a woman who said, *what shall I do with my antiques? I'm 80 years old and I've lived here for 28 years. What shall I do with my antiques?* Home to Charles Keenan and his wife, who put plastic not glass in their windows. Who had ragged curtains. Whose sink had a worn veneer. Whose sink produced hot and cold running water. Who read the newspaper in a wallpapered room. Who laid down tile in the kitchen and the bathroom. Who brewed coffee. Who shook out salt and pepper on their dinner. Who sat at a kitchen table facing a kitchen window looking out on the river. Parkerville, where men and women *sadly and silently contemplated their belongings, trying to decide what to take, what to leave behind, where to go.* Parkerville where men and women *stared bitterly at the condemnation signs tacked on their homes by the city.* Parkerville. Which had its mayor, too. A mayor who told the reporters who showed up for the bulldozers, *It's unfair to make us move. But you can't fight city hall.*

43.
Black and green clouds rolled into the city, punctuated
by scratches of lightning. And then the wind started to
blow. It sounded ten thousand bird wings flapping; it got
very dark, and there was a very fast wind, filled with leaves
and dirt. The clouds funneled down, and in less than 15
minutes, a tornado had chewed up 250 city blocks,
leaving collapsed buildings and fires and dead people and
dead horses everywhere. Lafayette Park, a few months
before the storm, still had a lake with fountains; the
tornado blew all the water off the lake, sent the swan boats
into actual flight (they landed in the street, miles away),
and collapsed the bandstand with the gold dome.
It shredded the Victorian gardens, symmetrical as argyle,
leaving nothing but tree stumps and stuff too heavy to
blow away—an iron bridge, two Revolutionary War
cannons, a statue of Thomas Hart Benton. Look at the
pictures. Look at them through a magnifying glass, at the
tiny faces, with no posing. You'll see people in shock, a
little boy rubbing his eye. The faces feel so modern they
seem almost banal. You'll see the corrosion of the
emulsion. You'll see the photo started to try to erase itself,
prognosticating damage. That botch on the surface of the
photo reminds you of some uncanny cavern, the kind of
place where a mad bear or a land wight might live. That
flaw will remind you most days are unremarkable, filled
with cooking and driving and licking bill envelopes shut.
But it says be ready for the rift, the fault line, when the
dullness of mowed grass and dry afternoon sunlight will
seem like the most precious thing in the world.

44.
Lambs arriving at the East St. Louis stockyards trotted into a 500-foot-long building with *Hotel de Sheep* painted over the door. It was well-drained and offered its residents sweet hay suspended from a wooden spindle; at capacity, it held 10,000 head. They printed a postcard where you could see the animals' mild faces, their jumbly configuration and two would-be Beau Brummel stockyard workers bending their jaunty canes against the feedlot floor—it felt more like a snapshot of a society ball than a slaughterhouse. You wonder if this picture was meant to connect the stockyards to East St. Louis' sparkling things: the soda- and glucose-works, the icehouses, the real society balls. In stockyards, of course, nothing sparkles, just glistens with metal or blood. These guys left the Hotel de Sheep through the canneries, the rendering plants and the carbon-works whose kiln reduced tons of animal bone to pounds of charcoal. Not even the smallest trace escaped: Baugh's Catch Basin, a huge apparatus on the bank of Cahokia Creek, even strained away *the superfluous grease that escaped through the sewer from the packing houses.* The joke was they canned everything but the pig's oink, but they couldn't steal the sheep's soul either. They trotted gently to the other world, like the pigs and sheep painted on the walls of catacombs wearing bells around their neck, or milk pails, suspended on a pastoral staff, over their unbreakable backs.

45.
This is a picture of my neighbor's father, born in 1931, year of the milk war. You think you know where those jokes came from, the jokes about the baby looking more like the milkman than dad. Everyone thinks it's because milkmen drove around the suburbs during the day while dad was at work. In Spain they tell *butaneros* jokes about the guys who deliver butane for the stove. Picture a milkman and I bet you see a guy in a blue zip-up jacket and a twee little hat to match. You see a man who wears a cap because he's a little thin on top and he wears a jacket to match not just to look official but because he can zip it up over his paunch. Picture a milkman and you picture a man in clompy, sensible shoes. A guy whose face has gone soft from a diet of curds and whey. But 1931 was a year marked by *the dumping of milk trucks, shooting from ambush, burning of cow barns and intimidation of anonymous threats.* The local press described it as a *bitter milk war,* so much crying over spilt milk, *close to guerrilla warfare,* like on a hot day in August when masked men highjacked an Effingham dairy farmer, pointed their guns, and ordered him to empty the tank. Two nights later a band of 40 masked men held up a milk tank truck from a rival dairy, not only dumping the milk, but burning the truck. What was a milkman to do but wear high black boots and fill his thermos with whiskey and tuck a knife or a gun into his waistband? What was a milkman to do but spend nights in his basement, doing sit-ups and pull-ups, thinking of himself as a dashing milk soldier? What was a milkman to do, but father children all across the city during the milk wars? And what was a milkman to do but keep driving his circuit, dropping glass bottles of whole milk on porches for all of his sons and daughters?

46.

If it had retained its original name, no one would play trombone in high school. Until the 18th century, the thing was called—brace yourself—a *sackbutt*. Variants included *shagbolt* and, even worse, *sagbutt*. What kid would dare carry a sag-butt case to school? It was the Italians who came up with the more mellifluous trombone (which the French stole, changing its definition to "paper clip"). In America, trombones play bright 'n' stripy Dixieland jazz, so we forget the instrument formerly known as the shagbolt was originally choral.
It symbolized death and the underworld. Though they'd never abide the old name, band kids—
who do not play football, who march to and fro across the AstroTurf in vinyl spats and shakos decorated with shredded-plastic plumes—gravitate toward that older darkness. Gargling on angst and hormones, emptying their spit valves, they imagine that long slide as their own cramped spirit unfolding, hoping, even if the sulfuric fumes turn the pennies in their loafers bright green, that one day they'll escape from hell.

47.

There's a tiny star splinter stuck in Jennifer's eye; she was born with it. She gets the same kind of migraines saints do. She was born with a diamond in her eye, a magic lens. When she's sick, she sees through walls and tells you what you're about to say. (Even people who don't know I'm Jennifer's sister call me Jennifer when they forget my name. She's a year younger. My parents were off in their naming and timing. She won't tell me what people call her when they forget that she's Jennifer.) My sister calls radio stations and wins tickets every time. She won't say if that's dumb luck or smart luck. She quilted a dress from all her backstage passes. She wears it to concerts, though it's so stiff she can't dance. (My father says when I was born he set me on his knee and asked, what's your name, little girl? And I made a noise and named myself. The saint with my name was the teenage wife of a soldier. She comforted St. Victor. They lashed her to two bent palms and cut the rope. I'm a Gemini. I've always lived on corners. I dream about rained-on maps, roads bleeding through both sides.) Jennifer found a loose diamond on the floor of a disco. *It strobed at me,* she said. *How could you miss it? It's easy to be lucky. You're not looking. You're not trying. You can't win if you don't enter.* (Negative ESP is real, I said, and I proved it: One month of scratch-offs, sweepstakes, crackerjacks, raffles, roulette, call-ins, ring toss, horseraces, bingo, bell jars, coin flips... I played, I played, I lost.) Jennifer flew to England. They were down to one engine over the ocean. Secret Jennifers shake or drink, but Actual Jennifers know their luck, and sleep. When there's a diamond floating in your eye, it fills your sight with the rainbows hiding in prisms. (My name means crown. What floats in my eye? A small cork heart and its shadow. A piece of wayward tinsel. A thistle seed. A fat green question mark. On the back of the retina, burnt image of my mother and father before I was born). My sister, cartwheeling to arrive right after. What's your secret? I ask her. *Rabbit, Rabbit,* she says.

Stefene Russell is a St. Louis-based poet, writer, editor and actor. She is a member of Poetry Scores, an arts collective dedicated to translating poetry into other media, including music, visual art, and food, and was Laumeier Sculpture Park's 2018 poet-in-residence. Her works include *Inferna* (2013, Intagliata Press) and *The Possum Codex* (2015, Otis Nebula). Find her online at stefenerussell.com.

Cover design by Philip P. Betts, using a digital version of the typeface Supersmoke (also known as No. 111), produced by William H. Page & Co. wood type company circa approximately 1891. A full set of this type is now in the collection of Central Print (centralprint.org), an arts non-profit in the Old North St. Louis neighborhood with a mission to promote the art of letterpress printmaking by providing workshops, classes, and programs focusing on design and production using historic printing equipment. Third-generation northsider Tom Bratkowski rescued Supersmoke—along with other wood typefaces and printing equipment—from the vacant offices of *Przewodnik Polski (Polish Guide)* in the early 1980s. The paper was one of dozens of non-English newspapers published throughout St. Louis between the 18th and 20th centuries. *Polish Guide's* final editor, Helen Muenz, inherited the paper from her mother, Helen Moczydlowski, who'd served as editor and publisher since 1905. In addition to reprinting syndicated news from overseas, the newspaper published news about St. Louis' Polish community, including births, deaths, weddings and neighborhood happenings. When Mrs. Muenz died in 1969, the paper ceased publication, and its headquarters—a two-family flat that contained not just the typesetting and printing equipment but the family's living spaces—stood empty for more than a decade. It was torn down in the mid-'80s and replaced with a Kentucky Fried Chicken. *Polish Guide* lives on as the *Hejnal*, a quarterly journal published by the Polish-American Cultural Society of Metropolitan St. Louis, whose masthead design was based on another wooden typeface saved from the *Polish Guide* offices.

This project was made possible, in part, by generous support from the Osage Arts Community.

Osage Arts Community provides temporary time, space and support for the creation of new artistic works in a retreat format, serving creative people of all kinds — visual artists, composers, poets, fiction and nonfiction writers. Located on a 152-acre farm in an isolated rural mountainside setting in Central Missouri and bordered by ¾ of a mile of the Gasconade River, OAC provides residencies to those working alone, as well as welcoming collaborative teams, offering living space and workspace in a country environment to emerging and mid-career artists. For more information, visit us at www.osageac.org

Osage Arts Community

www.ingramcontent.com/pod-product-compliance
Lightning Source LLC
Chambersburg PA
CBHW020127130526
44591CB00032B/558